SNAKES

North American Racer Snakes

by Adele D. Richardson

Consultants:
The staff of Black Hills Reptile Gardens
Rapid City, South Dakota

CAPSTONE
HIGH-INTEREST
BOOKS

an imprint of Capstone Press
Mankato, Minnesota

Capstone High-Interest Books are published by Capstone Press
151 Good Counsel Drive, P.O. Box 669, Mankato, Minnesota 56002
http://www.capstone-press.com

Library of Congress Cataloging-in-Publication Data
Richardson, Adele, 1966–
    North American racer snakes / by Adele D. Richardson.
    p. cm.—(Snakes)
    Summary: Describes the physical features, habitat, and hunting and mating
methods of North American racer snakes.
    Includes bibliographical references (p. 45) and index.
    ISBN 0-7368-2139-2 (hardcover)
    1. Racer snake—Juvenile literature. [1. Racer snake. 2. Snakes.] I. Title.
II. Series: Snakes (Mankato, Minn.)
QL666.O636R537 2004
597.96—dc21   2003000640

Editorial Credits

Tom Adamson, editor; Patrick Dentinger, book designer; Jo Miller, photo researcher

Photo Credits

Cover: blue racer; Root Resources/A. B. Sheldon

Allen Blake Sheldon, 10, 12, 33, 34
Animals Animals/Paul Freed, 14
Bruce Coleman Inc./E. R. Degginger, 6; James R. Simon, 9
Cathy & Gordon Illg, 40
Corbis/Eric & David Hosking, 16, 20
David Liebman, 28
James E. Gerholdt, 18–19, 26
Joe McDonald, 30, 36
Leonard Rue Enterprises, 22, 24, 38
Root Resources/A. B. Sheldon, 44

1 2 3 4 5 6 08 07 06 05 04 03

Table of Contents

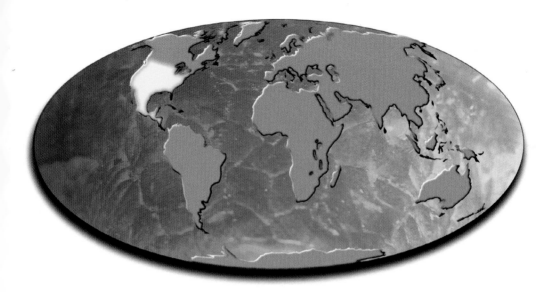

The yellow area shows where North American racer snakes live.

Fast Facts about Racers

Scientific Name: North American racer snakes belong to the genus *Coluber*. Their species name is *Coluber constrictor.*

Size: Most North American racers average between 3 and 6 feet (.9 and 1.8 meters) long.

Range: North American racers live throughout North America. They range from southern Canada to Central America.

Description:	Racers are slender, quick-moving snakes. Their tails look like whips. Adult racers can have black, blue, brown, or olive green on their backs. Their underbellies may be white, yellow, black, or dark gray.
Habitat:	North American racers live in prairies, along the edges of woods, and in deserts with shrubs. Some racers also live on rocky hillsides or along the edges of swamps and marshes.
Food:	Racers eat insects, birds, rodents, and frogs. They also eat lizards and other snakes.
Habits:	Racer snakes fight back roughly when they are handled. If picked up, they strike their handlers over and over. To warn predators, racers may shake their tails in a pile of leaves.
Reproduction:	North American racer snakes are oviparous. Female racers lay eggs that develop and hatch outside their bodies.

CHAPTER 1

North American Racer Snakes

Racer snakes earned their name because of how quickly they can move. When threatened, racers can travel about 8 miles (13 kilometers) per hour for short distances. This speed is about as fast as someone jogging.

Colubridae Family

Scientists divide snakes into families. North American racer snakes belong to the family Colubridae, the largest of the snake families. More than 1,800 species make up this group.

Racer snakes are slender and have smooth scales.

Rat snakes and garter snakes are some other members of Colubridae.

Most snakes in the Colubridae family are nonvenomous. North American racers are nonvenomous colubrids.

North American Racer Snake Genus

Scientists divide each snake family into genera. North American racers belong to the *Coluber* genus. The word *Coluber* means "serpent." More than 30 species are in this genus.

The North American racer's scientific name is *Coluber constrictor*. Most snakes with the name constrictor squeeze their prey to kill it. The racer does not kill prey this way. Scientists believe this snake was named by mistake. It may have been confused with the black rat snake, which constricts prey. Black rat snakes look similar to some racers.

There are 11 subspecies in the *Coluber constrictor* species. Many of the subspecies are different colors or have different types of scales. Some racers are part of a different

The eastern yellowbelly is one of 11 subspecies of racer snakes in North America.

subspecies because of where they live. For example, the eastern and western yellowbelly racers look alike. But the two subspecies live on different parts of the continent.

CHAPTER 2

Racer Subspecies

The 11 North American racer subspecies are between 3 and 6 feet (.9 and 1.8 meters) long. They have slender bodies with smooth, shiny scales. All racers have narrow heads and large eyes. The adults usually have an even color, but the young have color patterns and spots. Many racers are named for their color.

Black Racers

The northern black racer is mostly black. Its chin and throat have some white, and its eyes are red-brown. The young look very different from the adults. They are gray with brown or black blotches on their backs.

Northern black racers have an even black color.

The southern black racer looks similar to the northern black racer, but it has more white on its chin area. Its eyes can be red or orange. Young southern black racers are white and brown. Their color changes to black when they are about 2.5 feet (76 centimeters) long.

The blackmask racer is dark gray. Its underbelly is blue-gray. This snake was named for a black stripe around its eyes. The stripe makes the snake look like it is wearing a mask.

The brownchin racer is black like the northern and southern racers. The brownchin was named for the brown scales on its chin and lower jaw.

Colorful Racers

The buttermilk racer is another North American subspecies. Many are black or dark blue. These snakes have white, gray, or yellow spots all over their bodies. Other buttermilks are almost completely white with some black spots.

The blue racer's sides and back are pale blue or blue-green. The chin and throat area is white

Southern black racers look like northern black racers. They live in the southern part of the continent.

Tan racers get their name from their light brown color.

or yellow. Its underbelly is white, gray, or light blue. The young often have blotches of gray, brown, and red.

The eastern yellowbelly racer is blue, olive green, or light brown. Its throat is bright yellow. This racer's underbelly is white or yellow. Young yellowbellies are white or gray. They have red and brown blotches on their backs. Smaller red or brown spots appear on their bellies.

The western yellowbelly racer looks like the eastern yellowbelly. It is also blue, green, or brown and has a yellow underbelly. Young western yellowbellies are gray with red or brown blotches.

The tan racer is also named for its color. This light brown snake has lighter colored spots on its sides and back. This snake is found mostly in Texas.

Everglades and Mexican Racers

Some racers are named for where they live. The Everglades racer is found near the Everglades in southern Florida. This racer can be blue-gray, olive green, or brown. Its eyes are red or yellow. The snake's underbelly is white with gray or light blue spots.

The Mexican racer is also named for where it lives. It is common in Mexico and southern Texas. It is green or gray-green down the center of its back. The color is lighter on its sides. A Mexican racer's underbelly is yellow.

NORTH AMERICAN RACER SNAKE SUBSPECIES

common name   *scientific name*

blackmask racer - *Coluber constrictor latrunculus*

blue racer - *Coluber constrictor foxii*

brownchin racer - *Coluber constrictor helvigularis*

buttermilk racer - *Coluber constrictor anthicus*

eastern yellowbelly racer - *Coluber constrictor flaviventris*

Everglades racer - *Coluber constrictor paludicola*

Mexican racer - *Coluber constrictor oaxaca*

northern black racer - *Coluber constrictor constrictor*

southern black racer - *Coluber constrictor priapus*

tan racer - *Coluber constrictor etheridgei*

western yellowbelly racer - *Coluber constrictor mormon*

The Everglades racer lives only in Florida.

Eastern Yellowbelly Racer

Head

Tongue

Whip-like Tail

CHAPTER 3

Habitat

The 11 North American racer subspecies are found in many areas of the continent. Most North American racers live in the southern and eastern parts of the continent.

Where Racers Live

Three racer subspecies are found only in the southeastern United States. The Everglades racer lives only in Florida. The brownchin racer lives in Florida and Georgia. Southern black racers live in Florida, but they can be found as far north as North Carolina.

Several North American racers only live in the southern part of the continent. Mexican

Like other racers, the Everglades racer spends much of its time on the ground.

Racers are common in open areas. Blue racers are named for their pale green-blue color.

racers range from southern Texas to Central America. The tan, blackmask, and buttermilk racers live in Texas and Louisiana.

The most common racer in the West is the western yellowbelly. This snake is usually found west of the Rocky Mountains.

Two racer snake subspecies are found most often in the central part of the continent. The blue racer lives in the Great Lakes area. It is common from southern Ontario, Canada, to Illinois. The eastern yellowbelly's range is larger. It is found from Montana to Louisiana.

Habitat

There are only a few places North American racers do not live. They are not found high on mountains or in thick forests. They also stay away from northern Canada and other areas that get very cold. Racers do not live in hot deserts where there is no shelter.

North American racers are common in pastures, prairies, and other open areas. Many are found along the edges of forests. They also live in desert areas that have some shrubs.

Racers also live in damp areas and rocky places. They can be found near swamps and marshes. Some racers live near streams or along coastal areas. The snakes are also common on rocky hillsides.

Racers spend most of their time on the ground. They sometimes climb trees to hunt birds. They may also use trees for protection from predators. Hawks or larger snakes sometimes catch and eat racers.

CHAPTER 4

Hunting

North American racer snakes are carnivores. They hunt and eat other animals. Racers eat frogs, insects, birds, and birds' eggs. Mice, small squirrels, and other rodents are also prey. Racers sometimes even eat their own young.

Racer snakes are diurnal. They are active and hunt during the day, mostly in the morning. While hunting, they often travel with their heads raised several inches off the ground.

Senses for Hunting

North American racers' eyes are large and round. Scientists believe they can see better

The northern black racer raises its head off the ground while hunting.

Snakes flick their tongues out to collect scents.

than many other snakes. Racers seem to notice the slightest movement around them. They can also tell the difference between light and dark.

Racers, like other snakes, do not hear the same way people do. They do not have ears on the outside of their bodies. Racers use their whole bodies to feel sounds. As prey nears, the snakes feel the movement in the ground.

Racers have an organ on the roof of their mouths called the Jacobson's organ. Racers flick out their tongues a lot. The tongue collects scents in the air and on the ground. The tongue carries the scents to the Jacobson's organ. The organ helps the snakes smell prey. Males also use this organ to find females ready to mate.

Catching and Killing Prey

Racers chase prey. They grab the animal with their mouths. They eat insects, mice, and other small prey alive.

Racers grab large prey and hold it down. They use their bodies to press the prey to the ground. The snakes grab onto prey with their mouths. They hold on with their mouths as they make their way to the head so they can begin swallowing. This action makes racers look like they are chewing.

Racers, including this buttermilk racer, swallow prey headfirst.

Swallowing Prey

North American racers swallow prey whole. Most prey is swallowed headfirst. This action smothers living prey. The prey's legs fold up neatly inside the snake's body to make swallowing easier.

A racer can swallow prey larger than its mouth. A racer may eat a large frog or rat. Its upper and lower jaws are connected with ligaments. This stretchy tissue allows the snake to separate its jaws. Strong muscles then pull the prey from the snake's throat to its stomach.

A racer usually rests after eating so its food can digest. Strong acids are inside a racer's stomach. These liquids break down the food so the snake's body can use it. Digestion can take several days or longer. More time is needed to digest large prey. If the prey was small, racers hunt again soon.

CHAPTER 5

Mating

Many racer snakes hibernate all winter. Hibernation allows them to survive cold temperatures. When snakes hibernate, they lie very still. Their breathing and heartbeat slow down.

In spring, the snakes come out of hibernation. They begin searching for a mate. North American racers mate in April and May. When a female is ready to mate, she gives off a scent. A male racer detects this scent with his Jacobson's organ. He follows it until he finds a female racer.

A male racer uses its tongue to detect the scent of a female racer.

Courtship

Once the male racer finds a female, courtship begins. The male rubs his chin along the female's body. He flicks his tongue over her skin. Then the two snakes twist together for mating. The snakes may stay joined for a few minutes or for a few hours.

The male racer may spend several days trailing the female after mating. The trailing male follows the female wherever she goes. He tries to prevent the female from mating with another male. After a day or two, the male stops trailing. If the female is still giving off her scent, she may attract another male for mating.

Eggs

North American racer snakes are oviparous. About a month after mating, the females lay eggs. They may lay eggs in an old animal burrow or in a sawdust pile. Females also lay eggs in rotting tree stumps and logs. The rotting stumps and logs keep the eggs warm.

Racer eggs are soft and leathery.

Several female racers might lay their eggs in one place. They sometimes place their eggs with the eggs of another snake species. Racer eggs have been found with the eggs of ring-necked snakes and gopher snakes.

The young blue racer has spots all over its body. The spots fade as it becomes an adult.

Females lay between three and 28 white eggs at one time. The outsides are leathery. They stick together at first. They feel rough, as if salt were sprinkled on them. The eggs are 1 to 1.5 inches (2.5 to 3.8 centimeters) long. Young racers hatch from the eggs seven to eight weeks later.

Young

Young racer snakes use an egg tooth to cut an opening in the egg's leathery shell. An egg tooth is a tiny spur on a young snake's upper jaw. It falls off soon after hatching. The young can take from a few hours to a few days to completely leave the eggs.

Newly hatched racer snakes do not look like the adults. They are 7 to 14 inches (18 to 36 centimeters) long. Most young have more than one color. They have spots and patterns on their skin. The patterns fade as they get older. Young racers grow into their adult color when they reach about 20 inches (51 centimeters) long.

The young snakes are on their own as soon as they hatch. They must find their own food and shelter. Young racers usually eat insects and small frogs. They become adults at two to three years of age. A racer snake lives about 10 years in the wild.

CHAPTER 6

Racers and People

Some people keep snakes as pets. North American racers are not a good choice for pets. These snakes are aggressive. They will bite their handlers. Even though they are not venomous, the snakes have painful bites. Racers should only be handled by snake experts.

Myths

A common myth about snakes is that their skin is slimy. Some people believe this about racers because their scales are shiny. But racers actually have smooth, dry skin.

A snake's scales are smooth and dry.

The western yellowbelly and other racers climb trees to avoid predators.

Another myth says that racers are able to charm prey, especially birds. The birds cannot escape once they are charmed. But there is no proof that racers charm their prey. Many small animals become frozen with fear when they see a snake. But they are not charmed.

Another myth claims that rattlesnakes and racers are enemies. It says that racers attack and kill large rattlesnakes. Racers do kill and eat other snakes. But racers rarely attack snakes that are the same size or larger. They usually eat only smaller snakes.

Defenses

North American racer snakes defend themselves in several ways. Racers usually flee. They can move quickly through grass, in shrubs, and even up trees. The snakes often hide from predators under logs, leaves, or piles of rocks. They stay hidden until the danger passes.

To warn predators to stay away, racers make a buzzing sound. They shake their tails quickly in plants or a pile of leaves. This noise makes racers sound like rattlesnakes. If a predator still will not leave, the snakes bite at it.

If racers are captured, they fight back fiercely. Racers twist and thrash their bodies.

Racers in dry areas often eat lizards.

They also give off a bad odor and bite several times. They try to get a predator to drop them. Then they can quickly leave for shelter.

Racers may charge an enemy. A charging snake moves directly toward an animal or person that comes near. Racers rarely charge. Usually, racers only charge when their hibernation is disturbed. At most other times, they try to leave.

Benefits

North American racers are a benefit to people. They keep insect and rodent populations from getting too big.

Racers are especially important to farmers. Mice eat farmers' crops. They can also spread diseases. By eating these rodents, racers help to keep farmers' crops from becoming ruined. They also help prevent the spread of some diseases.

Words to Know

acids (ASS-ids)—substances in an animal's stomach that help it break down food

burrow (BUR-oh)—a hole in the ground made by an animal

carnivore (KAR-nuh-vor)—an animal that hunts other animals for food

constrict (kuhn-STRIKT)—to squeeze

digest (dye-JEST)—to break down food so it can be used by the body

diurnal (dye-UR-nuhl)—active during the day

family (FAM-uh-lee)—a group of animals with similar features

genus (JEE-nuhss)—a group of plants or animals that are related; genera is the plural of genus.

habitat (HAB-uh-tat)—the places and natural conditions in which a plant or animal lives

hibernate (HYE-bur-nate)—to be inactive during winter

ligament (LIG-uh-muhnt)—a strong, stretchy band of tissue that connects bones

oviparous (oh-VIP-uh-rus)—laying eggs that develop and hatch outside the female's body

predator (PRED-uh-tur)—an animal that hunts and eats other animals

prey (PRAY)—an animal that is hunted by another animal for food

species (SPEE-sheez)—a specific type of plant or animal

venom (VEN-uhm)—poison produced by some snakes

Blue Racer

To Learn More

Behler, Deborah, and John Behler. *Snakes.* Animalways. New York: Benchmark Books, 2001.

Berger, Melvin, and Gilda Berger. *Can Snakes Crawl Backward?: Questions and Answers about Reptiles.* Scholastic Question and Answer Series. New York: Scholastic Reference, 2001.

Greenaway, Theresa. *Snakes.* The Secret World Of. Austin, Texas: Raintree Steck-Vaughn, 2001.

Mattison, Christopher. *Snake.* New York: DK Publishing, 1999.

Mudd-Ruth, Maria. *Snakes.* Animals, Animals. New York: Marshall Cavendish, 2001.

Useful Addresses

Black Hills Reptile Gardens
P.O. Box 620
Rapid City, SD 57709

Chicago Herpetological Society
2430 North Cannon Drive
Chicago, IL 60614

The Minnesota Herpetological Society
The Bell Museum of Natural History
10 Church Street SE
Minneapolis, MN 55455-0104

Toronto Zoo
361A Old Finch Avenue
Scarborough, ON M1B 5K7
Canada

Internet Sites

Do you want to learn more about racers and other snakes?
Visit the FactHound at *http://www.facthound.com*

FactHound can track down many sites to help you. All
the FactHound sites are hand-selected by our editors.
FactHound will fetch the best, most accurate information
to answer your questions.

IT'S EASY! IT'S FUN!
1) Go to *http://www.facthound.com*
2) Type in: 0736821392
3) Click on "FETCH IT" and FactHound will put you on the
   trail of several helpful links.

You can also search by subject or book title. So, relax
and let our pal FactHound do the research for you!

Index